99 Great Guacamole Recipe

To Impress Your Friends

by Ann Sullivan

Published in USA by:

Ann Sullivan
217 N. Seacrest Blvd #9
Boynton Beach
FL 33425

© Copyright 2016

ISBN-13: 978-1539972396
ISBN-10: 1539972399

Table of Contents

Best Guacamole

INGREDIENTS

- 2 avocados
- 1/2 lemon, juiced
- 2 tbsps. onion, chopped
- 1/2 tsp. salt
- 2 tbsps. olive oil

DIRECTIONS

Slice the avocado in half, and take out the seed. Mash the avocado with lemon juice, onion, salt, and olive oil. Chill for 1 hour covered.

5-Minute Guacamole

INGREDIENTS

- 1 medium ripe avocado, peeled and cubed
- 1 tbsp. salsa
- 1 clove garlic, peeled
- 1/4 tsp. salt

DIRECTIONS

Blend all the ingredients together in a blender until smooth. Serve immediately or chilled.

Guacamole Cilantro Lime Cheeseburger

INGREDIENTS

Guacamole

- 2 avocados - halved, peeled, and pitted
- 1/2 lime, juiced
- 1 tsp. chili powder
- 1 fresh jalapeno peppers, seeded and minced
- 1/2 c. cilantro, chopped
- 1/4 c. onion, minced
- 1 1/2 tsps. garlic, minced
- 1/4 tsp. salt to taste

Burger

- 2 lbs. lean ground beef
- 1/2 lime, juiced
- 1 tbsp. garlic, minced
- 1/2 c. onion, diced
- 1/2 c. tomatoes, diced
- 6 slices Monterey Jack cheese

- 6 hamburger buns

DIRECTIONS

Heat a grill on medium heat.

In a medium bowl, mash the avocado with the juice slowly. Mix in chili powder, jalapeno, cilantro, ¼ cup onion, and 1 ½ tsp. minced garlic. Add salt to season.

In a separate bowl, add the juice slowly to the meat with 1 tbsp. garlic, ½ cup diced onion and tomatoes. Roll into 6 patties.

Grill the burgers until done, as desired. Serve on buns and top with cheese and guacamole.

Asparagus Guacamole

INGREDIENTS

- 24 spears fresh asparagus, trimmed and coarsely chopped
- 1/2 c. salsa
- 1 tbsp. cilantro, chopped
- 2 cloves garlic
- 4 green onions, sliced

DIRECTIONS

Bring the asparagus to a boil for 5 minutes. Drain and rinse under cold water.

In a blender, mix the asparagus, salsa, cilantro, garlic, and green onions until smooth. Chill for 1 hour.

Holiday Guacamole

INGREDIENTS

- 1/2 white onion, minced
- 4 serrano chile peppers, minced
- 1 tsp. kosher salt
- 4 avocados - peeled, pitted and diced
- 2 1/2 tbsps. fresh lime juice
- 1 pear - peeled, cored and diced
- 1 c. seedless green grapes, halved
- 1 c. pomegranate seeds

DIRECTIONS

Blend the onions, chile peppers, and salt before adding the avocados and lime juice to a bowl. Mix in the pear grapes and pomegranate. Let chill.

Grandpa's Guacamole

INGREDIENTS

- 2 avocados - peeled, pitted, and mashed
- 1/2 c. sour cream
- 2 tbsps. dry Ranch-style dressing mix

DIRECTIONS

Mix the avocado, sour cream, and dressing together in a bowl. Chill before serving.

Nicole's Avocado Dip

INGREDIENTS

- 1 (8 oz.) container cottage cheese
- 2 avocados - peeled, pitted, and mashed
- 1 (4 oz.) can green chilies, diced and drained
- salt and pepper to taste

DIRECbTIONS

Blend the cottage cheese, avocado, and chiles in a bowl.
Season with salt and pepper.

Citrus Infused Guacamole

INGREDIENTS

- 2 avocados - peeled, pitted, and mashed
- 1/2 tbsp. lime juice
- 1/2 tbsp. orange juice
- 1/2 tbsp. pineapple juice
- 1/4 tsp. ground cumin
- 1/4 c. cilantro, coarsely chopped
- salt to taste
- 1 tsp. hot pepper sauce, or to taste (optional)

DIRECTIONS

Blend the avocados with all the fruit juices, cumin, cilantro, and salt. Season with hot pepper. Chill before serving.

Basic Guacamole Dip

INGREDIENTS

- 4 ripe avocados - peeled, pitted, and mashed
- 2 tomatoes, diced
- 2 tbsps. onion, minced
- 1 tbsp. lemon juice

DIRECTIONS

Blend the avocado, tomato, onion, and lemon juice in a bowl until mixed well. Serve immediately, or chilled.

Guacamole Deviled Eggs

INGREDIENTS

- 4 whole eggs in the shell
- 2 avocados - peeled, pitted, and mashed
- 1 tbsp. cilantro, chopped
- 1 tbsp. green onion, minced
- 2 tsps. seeded jalapeno pepper, minced
- 2 tsps. fresh lime juice
- 1/2 tsp. salt, or to taste
- 1 dash hot pepper sauce (e.g. Tabasco™), or to taste
- 1 tsp. Worcestershire sauce, or to taste
- 1 tsp. Dijon-style prepared mustard
- 1 pinch paprika

DIRECTIONS

Bring eggs to a boil, then cover and let sit for 10 - 12 minutes off the heat. Once done, remove and cool to peel. Cut the eggs in half to remove the yolk.

In a bowl, mix the yolks with avocado, cilantro, green onion, and jalapeno. Pour in the lime juice. Use salt, hot sauce, Worcestershire sauce, and mustard to season. Once it is well blended, put mixture into each egg half. Garnish with paprika.

Tomauntilo Guacamole

INGREDIENTS

- 3 avocados - peeled, pitted, and mashed
- 3 tomauntilos, husked and chopped
- 1 red onion, finely chopped
- 3 roma (plum) tomatoes, seeded and chopped
- 1 tbsp. lime juice
- 1 tsp. red pepper flakes
- 3 drops hot pepper sauce
- salt and pepper to taste

DIRECTIONS

Blend the avocados with the tomauntilos, red onion, roma tomatoes, and lime juice in a medium bowl. Add red pepper flakes, hot pepper sauce, salt, and pepper to season. Chill for 45 minutes to serve.

LuAnn's Guacamole

INGREDIENTS

- 2 avocados - peeled, pitted and diced
- 2 tsps. salt
- 1 large tomato, diced
- 1 onion, diced
- 2 jalapeno peppers, chopped
- 1/2 tbsp. fresh cilantro, chopped
- 2 tbsps. fresh lime juice

DIRECTIONS

Mash the avocados with a fork. Season with salt. Add tomato, onion, jalapeno, cilantro, and lime juice. Chill covered for 30 minutes before serving.

Fabulous and Easy Guacamole

INGREDIENTS

- 2 avocados - peeled, pitted and diced
- 1 tbsp. shallots, minced
- 2 cloves garlic, minced
- 3/4 c. taco sauce

DIRECTIONS

Blend together the avocados, shallots, garlic, and taco sauce in a medium bowl. Set aside 15 minutes to let marinate.

Dave's Ultimate Guacamole

INGREDIENTS

- 4 avocados - peeled, pitted and sliced
- 1/2 c. salsa
- 1/4 tbsp. garlic powder
- 1/2 tsp. hot pepper sauce
- 1 pinch salt (optional)

DIRECTIONS

Blend avocados until lumpy in a processor, then add garlic powder and hot sauce. Blend until thick and smooth. Season with salt.

Gulf Coast Guacamole Dip

INGREDIENTS

- 4 ripe avocados - peeled, pitted, and mashed
- 1 1/2 c. picante sauce (such as Pace® Picante Sauce)
- 1 (4 oz.) can black olives, chopped
- 1 (8 oz.) carton sour cream
- 1/2 c. cooked small shrimp, chopped
- 1/2 tsp. seasoned salt (such as Morton® Nature's Seasons® Seasoning Blend).

DIRECTIONS

Mix the avocado, picante sauce, olives, sour cream, and shrimp together well. Use salt to season. Chill for 2 hours.

Green Stuff (Cucumber Guacamole)

INGREDIENTS

- 1 large avocado, peeled and pitted
- 1 tbsp. lime juice
- 2 green onions, chopped
- 1/2 cucumber, peeled and chopped
- 1/2 tsp. salt
- 1/2 c. cold water

DIRECTIONS

In a blender, mix together the avocado, lime juice, green onion, cucumber, salt, and water until smooth.

Grilled Guacamole

INGREDIENTS

- 4 Hass avocados, halved and pitted
- 1/2 c. red onion, diced
- 1 jalapeno pepper, seeded and minced
- 1/2 c. reduced-fat sour cream
- 2 tbsps. lime juice
- 1/2 tsp. garlic salt
- 1/2 tsp. hot pepper sauce (e.g. Tabasco™), or to taste
- 12 cherry tomatoes, quartered
- 2 tbsps. fresh cilantro, chopped

DIRECTIONS

Add oil and heat a grill on low heat.

Grill the avocados until they brown and caramelize

slightly. Cool, remove the skins, and cut into cubes. Add half of the avocado to a bowl. Mash with a fork while adding onion, jalapeno pepper, and sour cream. Pour in the lime juice and add garlic, salt, and hot pepper sauce. Mix in the remaining avocado, cherry tomatoes, and cilantro. Chill for 30 minutes.

BUSH'S® Black Bean Guacamole

INGREDIENTS

- 5 avocados, diced
- 3 scallions, chopped
- 2 limes, juiced
- 1/2 c. tomatoes, chopped
- 1 tbsp. cilantro, chopped
- 1 (15 oz.) can BUSH'S® Black Beans, drained and rinsed
- Salt and black pepper to taste
- Assorted dippers such as toasted whole wheat pita bread triangles or multi-grain tortilla chips.

DIRECTIONS

Mash together the avocados, scallions, and lime juice in a bowl. Add tomatoes, cilantro, and beans. Season with salt and pepper to taste. Serve.

Gourmet Guacamole

INGREDIENTS

- 2 avocados, chopped
- 2 tbsps. salsa
- 2 tbsps. mayonnaise
- 1/4 tsp. chili powder
- 1/4 tsp. ground black pepper
- salt to taste

DIRECTIONS

Blend the avocados, salsa, mayonnaise, chili powder, and black pepper together in a bowl well. Season with salt and serve.

Sheila's Greek Style Avocado Dip

INGREDIENTS

- 1 avocado - peeled, pitted and diced
- 1 clove garlic, minced
- 2 tbsps. lime juice
- 1 roma (plum) tomato, seeded and diced
- 1/4 c. crumbled feta cheese

DIRECTIONS

Use a fork to mash the avocado, garlic, and lime juice until smooth. Add the tomato and feta cheese to serve.

Mexican Guacamole

INGREDIENTS

- 3 avocados, peeled and mashed
- 1 red onion, minced
- 1 red bell pepper, chopped
- 1/2 yellow bell pepper, chopped
- 1 green bell pepper, chopped
- 1 fresh jalapeno pepper, chopped
- 1/3 c. fresh cilantro, chopped
- 1 lime, juiced

DIRECTIONS

Blend the avocados, onion, bell peppers, jalapenos, and cilantro with lime juice in a bowl. Blend well, then chill covered before serving.

Simply Guacamole

INGREDIENTS

- 5 avocados - peeled, pitted, and mashed
- 2 tbsps. fresh lemon juice
- 3/4 green onion, minced
- 1/2 c. fresh cilantro, minced
- salt and pepper, to taste

DIRECTIONS

In a bowl, mix the avocado and lemon juice until smooth. Mix in green onion, and cilantro. Add salt and pepper to taste. Chill or serve immediately.

Fresh Guacamole

INGREDIENTS

- 1 avocado - peeled, pitted, and diced
- 1 roma (plum) tomato, diced
- 1/2 red onion, diced
- 1 serrano chile pepper, seeded and minced
- 1/2 tsp. kosher salt
- 1/2 tsp. ground black pepper
- 1/2 tsp. garlic powder
- 1 tsp. Worcestershire sauce
- 3 drops hot sauce
- 6 cilantro leaves, minced
- 1 tbsp. fresh lime juice

DIRECTIONS

Blend together the avocado, tomato, onion, serrano chile, salt, pepper, garlic powder, Worcestershire sauce, hot sauce, and cilantro. Add lime juice to the top. Chill or serve.

Daddy's Guacamole Dip

INGREDIENTS

- 2 avocados, halved with pits removed
- 2 tomatoes, diced
- 1 jalapeno pepper, seeded and minced
- 1/2 c. sweet onion, diced
- 1 lemon, juiced
- 2 c. cottage cheese
- 1/2 tsp. garlic powder
- salt and pepper to taste

DIRECTIONS

Mash the avocado with lemon juice. Add tomatoes, jalapeno pepper, onion, cottage cheese, garlic powder, salt, and pepper. Stir well. Chill for 1 hour.

California Guacamole with Bacon

INGREDIENTS

- 4 ripe avocados - peeled, pitted, and mashed
- 4 slices bacon, cooked until crisp, drained and crumbled
- 1 large tomato, seeded and finely chopped
- 1 onion, finely chopped
- 1 clove garlic, minced
- salt and pepper to taste
- 1 dash hot pepper sauce to taste (optional)

DIRECTIONS

In a bowl, mash the avocados. Add bacon, tomatoes, onion, and garlic. Use salt and pepper to season. Pour in hot pepper sauce to taste. Serve.

Fruity Guacamole

INGREDIENTS

- 1 avocado - peeled, pitted, and diced
- 1 1/2 tsps. red onion, minced
- 1 tsp. seeded serrano chile, minced
- 12 red grapes, halved
- 1/2 c. fresh peaches, diced
- salt to taste
- 2 tbsps. pomegranate seeds (optional)

DIRECTIONS.

Mash avocado with onion and serrano pepper. Add grapes and peaches. Use salt to season. Serve garnished with pomegranate seeds.

Guacamole

INGREDIENTS

- 3 avocados - peeled, pitted, and mashed
- 1 lime, juiced
- 1 tsp. salt
- 1/2 c. onion, diced
- 3 tbsps. fresh cilantro, chopped
- 2 roma (plum) tomatoes, diced
- 1 tsp. garlic, minced
- 1 pinch ground cayenne pepper (optional)

DIRECTIONS

Blend avocado, lime juice, and salt together well in a bowl. Add onion, cilantro, tomatoes, and garlic. Season with cayenne pepper, and chill for 1 hour.

Tucson Guacamole

INGREDIENTS

- 1 (8 oz.) package cream cheese, softened
- 2 large ripe avocados, peeled and pitted
- 1 (4 oz.) can green chiles, diced and drained
- 2 tsps. Worcestershire sauce, or to taste
- garlic salt to taste
- black pepper to taste
- 1 large ripe avocado, peeled and pitted

DIRECTIONS

Use an electric mixer to beat the cream cheese until it is smooth. Blend in the avocados, green chiles, Worcestershire sauce, garlic, salt, and pepper. Mix until smooth.

Easy Guacamole

INGREDIENTS

- 2 avocados
- 1 small onion, finely chopped
- 1 clove garlic, minced
- 1 ripe tomato, chopped
- 1 lime, juiced
- salt and pepper to taste

DIRECTIONS

Mash the avocados with onion, garlic, tomato, lime juice, salt, and pepper. Use the lime juice, salt, and pepper to season. Chill for ½ hour.

Chipotle Guacamole

INGREDIENTS

- 2 avocados, peeled, seeded and cubed
- 1 tbsp. fresh lime juice
- 2 tbsps. sour cream
- 1/4 c. salsa, or to taste
- 1/4 tsp. adobo sauce from canned chilies, or to taste
- salt and pepper to taste

DIRECTIONS

Blend the avocado, lime juice, sour cream, salsa, and adobo sauce well in a bowl. Use salt and pepper to season.

Cucumber Guacamole

INGREDIENTS

- 1 large avocado, peeled and pitted
- 1 tbsp. lime juice
- 2 green onions, chopped
- 1/2 cucumber, peeled and chopped
- 1/2 tsp. salt
- 1/2 c. cold water

DIRECTIONS

Mix avocado, lime juice, green onion, cucumber, salt, and water until smooth in a processor or blender.

Chipotle Guacamole II

INGREDIENTS

- 2 avocados, peeled, seeded and cubed
- 1 tbsp. fresh lime juice
- 2 tbsps. sour cream
- 1/4 c. salsa, or to taste
- 1/4 tsp. adobo sauce from canned chilies, or to taste
- salt and pepper to taste

DIRECTIONS

Blend the avocado, lime juice, sour cream, salsa, and adobo sauce together well. Season to taste with salt and pepper.

Easiest, Amazing Guacamole

INGREDIENTS

- 2 (6 oz.) avocados, pitted peeled and mashed
- 1/4 tsp. coarse garlic salt

DIRECTIONS

Mix the avocado with garlic salt until smooth.

Halloween Brain Dip

INGREDIENTS

- 2 avocados
- 1/2 c. prepared salsa
- 1 head cauliflower
- 6 thin slices red and blue fruit leather

DIRECTIONS

Cut and remove the avocado from the skin. Mash with salsa, and set aside. Slice the avocado pit in half.
Take the leaves and stems off the cauliflower. Leave head intact with a hollow area in the middle. Fill the hollow with avocado dip, and use the pits to make eyes. Weave red and blue fruit between florets to create veins and arteries.

Muir Glen® Salsa Guacamole

INGREDIENTS

Salsa:

- 1 (14.5 oz.) can Muir Glen® organic fire roasted or plain tomatoes, diced and well drained
- 1/4 c. onion, chopped
- 2 tbsps. fresh cilantro, chopped
- 1/4 tsp. coarse salt (kosher or sea salt)
- 1 clove garlic, finely chopped
- 1 small fresh jalapeno chile, seeded, finely chopped
-

Guacamole:

- 3 large ripe avocados, pitted, peeled
- 2 tbsps. fresh lime juice
- 1/2 tsp. coarse salt (kosher or sea salt)
- 1/2 tsp. red pepper sauce
- 1 clove garlic, finely chopped

DIRECTIONS

Mix all ingredient for the salsa in a medium bowl.

In a separate bowl, mash the avocados and add remaining ingredients. Put in a bowl and top with salsa.

Guacamole Salad Bowl

INGREDIENTS

- 5 c. torn leaf lettuce
- 2 medium tomatoes, cut into wedges
- 1 c. Cheddar cheese, shredded
- 1 c. salad shrimp, cooked
- 1 c. corn chips
- 1/2 c. ripe olives, sliced
- 1/4 c. green onions, sliced
- AVOCADO DRESSING:
- 1/2 c. ripe avocado, mashed
- 1 tbsp. lemon juice
- 1/2 c. sour cream
- 1/3 c. vegetable oil
- 1 garlic clove, minced
- 1/2 tsp. sugar
- 1/2 tsp. chili powder
- 1/4 tsp. salt
- 1/4 tsp. hot pepper sauce

DIRECTIONS

Mix the first 7 ingredients together. Lay to the side for later. Blend all dressing ingredients until smooth. Toss with the salad and serve.

Creamy Guacamole

INGREDIENTS

- 1 medium ripe avocado - halved, seeded and peeled
- 2 tsps. lime juice
- 2 (3 oz.) packages cream cheese, softened
- 1/2 tsp. Worcestershire sauce
- 1/4 tsp. salt
- 1/4 tsp. hot pepper sauce
- Tortilla chips

DIRECTIONS

Blend the avocado with lime juice, and beat in cream cheese. Add Worcestershire sauce, salt, and hot pepper. Blend until smooth.

Salsa Guacamole

INGREDIENTS

- 6 ripe avocados, halved, pitted and peeled
- 1/4 c. lemon juice
- 1 c. salsa
- 2 green onions, finely chopped
- 1/4 tsp. salt or salt-free seasoning blend
- 1/4 tsp. garlic powder
- Tortilla chips

DIRECTIONS

Mix avocado and lemon juice in a bowl until smooth.
Add salsa, onions, salt, and garlic powder. Serve.

Simple Guacamole

INGREDIENTS

- 2 medium ripe avocados
- 1 tbsp. lemon juice
- 1/4 c. chunky salsa
- 1/8 tsp. salt

DIRECTIONS

Coarsely mash the avocados with lemon juice, salsa, and salt. Chill to serve.

Charred Tomatillo Guacamole

INGREDIENTS

- 6 oz. tomatillos (6 or 7), husked and rinsed
- 1/2 small red onion, finely chopped
- 3 to 4 fresh serrano chiles, seeded (optional) and finely chopped
- 1/2 c. finely fresh cilantro, chopped
- 1 tsp. salt
- 1/2 tsp. black pepper
- 2 large California avocados (1 lb. total)

DIRECTIONS

In a baking pan, broil the tomatillos for 7 - 10 minutes until charred. Turn, and char for 5 more minutes.

Mix together onion, chiles, cilantro, salt, and pepper in a bowl. Slowly add the tomatillos, and mash. Mash in the avocados so that it remains chunky but well mixed.

Mango Pomegranate Guacamole

INGREDIENTS

* 4 ripe avocados (2 lbs. total)
* 1 c. white onion, finely chopped
* 2 fresh serrano chiles, finely chopped (2 tbsps.), including seeds
* 1/4 c. fresh lime juice, or to taste
* 3/4 c. pomegranate seeds (from 1 pomegranate)
* 3/4 c. peeled mango, diced
* 1/2 c. cilantro, chopped
* Accompaniment: plantain chips
* Garnish: lime wedges

DIRECTIONS

Blend the avocados in a bowl until smooth. Mix in onion, chiles, ¼ cup lime juice, and 1 ¼ tsp. salt. Mix together well, then add pomegranate seeds, mango, and cilantro. Use salt and lime juice to season to taste.

Guacamole II

INGREDIENTS

- 2 ripe California avocados (1 lb. total), quartered, pitted, and peeled
- 1/2 c. fresh cilantro, chopped
- 1/2 c. white onion, minced
- 1 fresh serrano chile including seeds, minced
- 2 tsps. fresh lime juice, or to taste
- 1 1/2 tsps. kosher salt, or to taste
- 3/4 to 1 c. cold water

DIRECTIONS

In a bowl, mash all the ingredients together until smooth. Add water to reach desired consistency.

Guacamole with Fresh Corn and Chipotle

INGREDIENTS

- 2 large ripe avocados (about 1 1/2 lbs.), halved, pitted, peeled
- 1 tbsp. fresh lime juice
- 1 ear of fresh corn
- 1 plum tomato, seeded, diced
- 2 green onions, chopped
- 1 canned chipotle chile, finely chopped*
- 1/4 c. sour cream

DIRECTIONS

In a medium bowl, mash together the avocados and lime juice. Take the kernels off the cob to mix into avocado mixture. Add tomato and green onions. In a separate bowl, mix chipotle and sour cream. Add to guacamole mixture. Use salt to season. Chill.

Guacamole con Frutas

INGREDIENTS

- 1 avocado (preferably Hass), diced
- 1/2 tbsp. red onion, minced
- 1 tsp serrano chile, minced
- 12 black or red grapes, halved
- 1/2 c. peaches (or mangoes), diced
- Pomegranate seeds (optional)

DIRECTIONS

In a bowl, mash the avocado, onion, and chile so that it is lumpy. Add grapes and peaches. Season with salt to taste. Serve garnished with pomegranate seeds.

Asparagus Guacamole and Chips

INGREDIENTS

- 1 medium Anaheim chile (or for extra heat, 1 serrano chile)
- 1 tsp olive oil
- 5 or 6 fresh asparagus spears, ends trimmed
- 1/2 c. nonfat plain yogurt
- 2 medium avocados, cut into cubes (about 2 c.)
- 1 plum tomato, seeded and diced
- 1 tbsp. green onion, chopped
- 1/4 c. fresh cilantro, chopped
- 1 tbsp. fresh lime juice (or more to taste)
- Dash garlic powder
- 1/2 tsp salt
- 1/2 tsp freshly ground black pepper
- Baked tortilla chips

DIRECTIONS

Protect your skin by wearing gloves. Heat a broiler. Coat

chile with oil to broil each side for 5 minutes until charred. Seal in a plastic bag to steam for 10 minutes. Remove the stem, skin, and seeds of the chile, and dice.

In a pan, bring water to a boil. Add ice water to a medium bowl. Boil the asparagus for 3 to 4 minutes, and plunge into ice water. Cool, dry, and chop into 1 inch pieces. Blend in a processor and mix in yogurt and avocado until smooth. Add remaining ingredients to serve.

Guacamole with Lime and Roasted Chilies

INGREDIENTS

- 3 poblano chilies* (about 12 oz.)
- 1 large jalapeño chili
- 8 tbsps. fresh lime juice
- 1 large plum tomato, seeded, chopped
- 2 small green onions, finely chopped
- 1 tsp. lime peel, grated
- 2 large ripe avocados, peeled, pitted
- 2/3 c. onion, finely chopped
- 1/2 c. (packed) fresh cilantro, coarsely chopped
- 1/4 tsp. ground cumin

DIRECTIONS

Char the chilies over a flame until blackened. Put in a bag to steam for 10 minutes to 1 hour. Remove peel, seeds, and dice the chilies. Blend with 1 tbsp. lime juice, tomato, green onions, and lime peel. Use salt to season.

In a processor, puree the next 4 ingredients with 7 tbsps. of lime juice until smooth. Add salt to season.

Add chili mixture to center of avocado mixture in a bowl to serve.

Guacamole with Pear and Pomegranate Seeds

INGREDIENTS

- 1/3 c. white onions, finely chopped
- 3 to 4 serrano chiles, finely chopped, with seeds
- 1 tsp. coarse salt
- 2 lbs. ripe California avocadoes (about 4 large)
- 2 to 3 tbsps. fresh lime juice
- 3/4 c. pear, peeled and finely diced
- 3/4 c. seedless grapes, halved
- 3/4 c. pomegranate seeds

DIRECTIONS

Puree onion, chiles, and salt into a paste in a food processor. Mash in the avocados one at a time. Pour in lime juice and stir. Add pear, grapes, and ½ cup pomegranate seeds. Top with pomegranate seeds to serve.

Guacamole with Tomatoes, Cilantro and Jalapenos

INGREDIENTS

4 ripe large avocados, peeled, pitted 1/2 c. finely chopped onion

- 4 ripe large avocados, peeled, pitted
- 1/2 c. onion, finely chopped
- 1/2 c. seeded plum tomatoes, chopped
- 1/2 c. fresh cilantro, chopped
- 1 4-oz. can mild green chilies, diced and drained
- 1 to 2 tsps. seeded jalapeño chilies, finely chopped

DIRECTIONS

In a large bowl, mash the avocados with a fork. Add onion, tomatoes, cilantro, and canned chilies. Blend in desired amount of jalapeno peppers. Add salt and pepper to season. Chill to serve.

Chunky Guacamole

INGREDIENTS

- 5 radishes
- 1 small white or sweet onion
- 2 fresh jalapeño chiles
- 1/2 c. packed fresh cilantro sprigs
- 4 firm-ripe California avocados
- 4 tbsps. fresh lime juice, or to taste
- 1/2 tsp. salt

DIRECTIONS

Slice ¼ inch thick slices from outside of radishes, and discard the middle portions. Dice radish and onion into ¼ inch pieces. Seed and chop the jalapeno. Cut up the cilantro into pieces. Mash the avocado with radish, onion, chiles, cilantro, lime juice, and salt.

Guacamole III

INGREDIENTS

- 2 plum tomatoes
- 2 firm-ripe California avocados
- 2 tbsps. red onion, minced
- 3 tbsps. fresh lime juice
- 1 tsp. garlic, minced

DIRECTIONS

Slice the tomatoes into quarters, and remove the seeds. Dice the tomatoes. Remove the pit from the avocado to scoop out the flesh. Use a fork to mash the avocado, and then add tomatoes and all other ingredients. Season with salt and pepper.

Tomato, Cucumber and Guacamole Sandwiches

INGREDIENTS

- 1/2 large avocado, peeled
- 1 tbsp. fresh lime juice
- 1 garlic clove, pressed
- 1 tsp. jalapeno & tilde chili, minced
- 8 slices good-quality whole wheat bread (each about 4x4 inches and 1/2 inch thick)
- 20 thin tomato slices
- 16 thin cucumber slices, peeled
- 8 thin red onion slices
- 1 c. lightly packed fresh cilantro sprigs

DIRECTIONS

Blend together the avocado, lime juice, garlic, and jalapeno until smooth. Add salt and pepper to season.

Spread mixture over bread slices evenly. Top each with 5

tomato slices, 4 cucumber slices, 2 onion slices, and cilantro. Press another bread slice over the top to make a sandwich. Cut and serve.

Guacamole IV

INGREDIENTS

- 3 ripe avocados
- 2 fresh serrano chilies
- 3 tbsps. white onion, finely chopped
- coarse salt to taste

DIRECTIONS

Slice the chilies up into small pieces and mash with avocados, onion, and salt. Chill for up to 2 hours before serving.

Light and Creamy Guacamole

INGREDIENTS

- 1 1/2 c. plain nonfat yogurt
- 1 large ripe avocado, peeled, pitted,
- 1/4 c. green onions, chopped
- 1/4 c. fresh cilantro, chopped
- 1 tsp. fresh lemon juice
- 1/4 tsp. ground cumin
- 3 carrots, peeled, sliced diagonally
- 1 small jicama, peeled, cut into 1/4-inch-thick triangles
- 1 bunch radishes, trimmed and sliced
- Fresh cilantro sprigs

DIRECTIONS

Place cheesecloth over a bowl and strain the yogurt while chilling overnight.

Drain liquid, and blend yogurt with avocado and next four ingredients in a processor until smooth. Add salt and pepper to season. Chill and serve garnished with cilantro. Serve with vegetables.

Authentic Guacamole

INGREDIENTS

- 2 ripe California avocados
- 3 serrano chiles* with seeds, minced, or 1 fresh jalapeño chile with seeds, minced (wear rubber gloves)
- 1/8 tsp. coarse salt, or to taste

DIRECTIONS

Mash the avocados with chiles. Use salt to season before serving.

Chicken and Black-Bean Guacamole Tostadas

INGREDIENTS

- 1 large ripe avocado, peeled, pitted
- 4 tsps. fresh lime juice
- 2/3 c. canned black beans, rinsed, drained
- 2 green onions, chopped
- Hot pepper sauce (such as Tabasco)
- 2 cooked chicken breast halves, shredded (about 1 3/4 c.)
- 1 tomato, seeded, chopped
- 2 tbsps. fresh cilantro, chopped
- 1 tsp. ground cumin
- Lime juice
- 4 purchased tostada shells (crisp corn tortillas)
- 2 c. lettuce, shredded
- 2/3 c. crumbled mild goat cheese (such as Montrachet) or feta cheese
- Purchased salsa

DIRECTIONS

Mash avocados with lime juice in a bowl. Add beans and green onions. Season with hot sauce, salt, and pepper. Mix the shredded chicken with tomato, cilantro, and cumin in a separate bowl. Season with lime juice, salt, and pepper.

Top tostadas with lettuce, guacamole, and chicken mixture. Add goat cheese and salsa to the top.

Guacamole with Scallion and Coriander

INGREDIENTS

- 3 avocados (preferably California)
- 1/4 c. scallion, finely chopped
- 1/4 c. fresh coriander, finely chopped
- 2 tbsps. fresh lemon juice, or to taste
- tortilla chips as an accompaniment
- cherry peppers for garnish if desired

DIRECTIONS

Mash the avocados with the scallion, coriander, and lemon juice. Season with salt. Chill before serving.

New Wave Guacamole

INGREDIENTS

- 2 ripe avocados, peeled, pitted
- 3 tbsps. fresh lime juice
- 2 tbsps. fresh ginger, minced
- 1 tbsp. seeded jalapeño or serrano chili, chopped
- 2 tsps. Garlic, minced
- 1 tsp. curry powder
- Peanut oil
- 1 12-oz. package wonton wrappers
- 1 c. cucumber, diced, peeled, and seeded
- 1/4 c. fresh cilantro, chopped

DIRECTIONS

Mash the first 6 ingredients in a bowl. Chill.

Add 3 inches of oil to a saucepan and heat to 375 degrees. Slice the wontons in half to form triangles. Fry each for 30 seconds so that they turn crisp. Drain on a paper towel, and season with salt.

Add cucumber and cilantro to guacamole. Use salt and pepper to season. Serve with fried wonton chips.

Spicy Guacamole

INGREDIENTS

- 1 large ripe avocado, peeled, pitted
- 2 tsps. fresh lime juice
- 1/2 c. fresh cilantro, chopped
- 1/4 c. onion, finely chopped
- 2 large garlic cloves, finely chopped
- 2 large serrano chilies seeded, chopped
- 1/4 tsp. salt

DIRECTIONS

Blend the avocado and lime juice together in a small bowl. Mix in the cilantro, onion, garlic, serrano chilies, and salt. Mix well before serving.

Guacamole V

INGREDIENTS

- 2 ripe avocados (preferably California)
- 1 small onion, minced
- 1 garlic clove, minced and mashed to a paste with 1/2 tsp. salt
- 4 tsps. fresh lime juice, or to taste
- 1/2 tsp. ground cumin
- 1 fresh or pickled jalapeño chili if desired, seeded and minced (wear rubber gloves)
- 3 tbsps. fresh coriander, chopped

DIRECTIONS

Coarsely mash the avocados with onion, garlic paste, lime juice, cumin, chili, and coriander. Chill for up to 2 hours before serving.

Tomatoes Stuffed with Guacamole

INGREDIENTS

- 12 small (2- to 2 1/2-inch) tomatoes (not plum tomatoes)
- 1 tbsp. olive oil
- 1 tbsp. fresh lime juice
- 3 firm-ripe California avocados
- 2 tbsps. Onion, finely chopped
- 1/2 tsp. fresh cilantro, finely chopped
- 2 tsps. fresh jalapeño chile, including seeds, minced
- 1/2 tsp. salt
- Accompaniment: iceberg lettuce, shredded
- Garnish: fresh cilantro sprigs

DIRECTIONS

Make cups out of the tomatoes by slice off the top, and scooping out the contents. Chop the pulp up.

Drip oil and lime juice into each tomato cup, and set aside.

Mash the avocados, and add the tomato pulp, onion, cilantro, chile, and salt. Serve in the tomato bowls.

Gorditas

INGREDIENTS

- 1 8.25-oz. can creamed corn
- 1/2 tsp. salt
- 2/3 c. cornmeal
- 1 tbsp. unsalted butter
- 1/2 c. queso añejo (or Jack cheese)

DIRECTIONS

Filling of choice:
- Shredded rotisserie chicken (or cooked pork), beans, shredded lettuce, extra cheese, chopped tomatoes, sliced radish, sour cream, guacamole

Heat the oven to 400 degrees.

Mix together the corn, salt, and ½ cup water in a pan

over medium heat. Stir in cornmeal, and cook for 5 minutes so that the liquid is absorbed.

Blend in butter and cheese, and remove for heat.

Grease a muffin pan, and add the mixture over 6 cups. Press and bake for 20 to 25 minutes. Cool for 5 minutes, and then stuff with desired filling.

Fajitas

INGREDIENTS

- Skirt Steak Fajita strips
- Chicken Fajita strips
- 2 to 4 c. tomatoes, diced
- 2 or 3 large onions, thinly slivered
- 4 limes, quartered
- 1/4 c. flat-leaf parsley or cilantro, chopped for garnish
- 16 flour tortillas (7 1/2-inch diameter), warmed
- Tomato Papaya Salsa
- 2 to 4 c. guacamole, store-bought or homemade
- 2 to 3 c. sour cream
- 2 to 3 c. grated Monterey Jack

DIRECTIONS

Decorate a platter with the steak, chicken, tomatoes,

onions, and lime. Top with parsley.

Warm the tortillas, and add to a basket. Add all other toppings to separate bowls.

Fill tortillas with desired toppings, roll, and serve.

GUACAMOLE VI

INREDIENTS

- 1 ripe tomato, peeled
- 2 avocados
- 1/2 onion, minced
- 1 tbsp. vinegar
- 1 green chile, chopped
- salt and pepper to taste

DIRECTIONS

Blend the tomato and avocados together in a bowl. Mix in all remaining ingredients, and serve.

GRILL ROASTED GREEN CHILES STUFFED WITH GUACAMOLE

INGREDIENTS

- 8 Anaheim or long green chiles
- olive oil
- 4 ripe Haas avocados
- 4 ripe medium tomatoes, halved, seeded, and coarsely chopped
- 1 small onion, finely chopped
- 2 cloves garlic, minced
- 3 small scallions (white and green parts), finely chopped
- 3/4 c. fresh cilantro, chopped
- 3 tbsps. lime juice
- 1 small jalapeno, seeded and finely chopped
- kosher salt and freshly ground black pepper

DIRECTIONS

Heat the grill, and brush oil over the chiles to grill for 15 minutes until blackened. Steam by closing them in a bag for 10 minutes. Remove the skin, and add ½ slits. Take out the seed, but leave the ribs.

Make the guacamole by blending avocado, tomatoes, onion, garlic, scallions, lime juice, and jalapenos until smooth. Season with salt and pepper. Serve by spooning into the chiles.

ZESTY GUACAMOLE

INGREDIENTS

- 2 avocados
- 1 medium tomato
- 1 tbsp. lime juice
- 1 tsp. onion powder
- 1/2 tsp. salt

DIRECTIONS

Dice ½ the tomato. Mix with the avocado, salt, lime juice, and onion powder until it reaches a desired consistency.

NICOLE'S AMAZING GUACAMOLE

INGREDIENTS

- 4 avocados
- 2 tbsp. olive oil
- 1/2 sm. Onion, minced
- 2 sm. cloves garlic, minced
- 1 sm. Tomato, finely chopped
- 1 tbsp. cilantro, finely chopped
- 1/2 tsp. cumin
- 1/2 c. sour cream
- 1 tbsp. lime juice
- 1 tsp. red pepper flake (to taste)
- salt and pepper
- shot of hot sauce

DIRECTIONS

Mash all ingredients together well, and serve.

VEGETABLE GUACAMOLE

INGREDIENTS

- 1 avocado, mashed
- 4 pieces of lettuce, chopped
- 1 peeled celery stick, chopped
- 1 cube frozen garlic, melted
- 1 frozen artichoke heart, cooked and chopped

DIRECTIONS

Mash the avocado and lettuce together well. Add all remaining ingredients, and then serve.

REALLY EASY GUACAMOLE

INGREDIENTS

- 4 small avocados, peeled and mashed
- 1 can Mexican Rotel, drained
- 8 oz. sour cream
- 1 small red onion, chopped
- 1 tsp. garlic powder (or to taste)
- 1 tsp. cumin powder (or to taste)
- salt, to taste
- juice of one lime

DIRECTIONS

Blend all the ingredients together, and then chill before serving.

GUACAMOLE BEAN CASSEROLE DIP

INGREDIENTS

- 1 can refried beans (spicy if desired)
- 1 can green chiles, chopped
- 1 1/2 c. guacamole, chilled
- 1 jar Ortega green chili salsa
- Grated Cheddar cheese (Optional: Mozzarella cheese mixed with Cheddar)

DIRECTIONS

Heat the beans and ½ can of green chiles in a small pan. Add layers of beans, guacamole, salsa, and chiles to a casserole dish. Sprinkle with cheese to serve.

GUACAMOLE SALSA

INGREDIENTS

- 4 perfectly ripe avocados
- 1 tbsp. fresh lemon juice
- 1/4 c. your own homemade salsa (any kind) or store bought salsa
- 1/4 c. sour cream, plain yogurt, or crème fraiche
- 1 tbsp. onion, grated
- Garlic salt to taste
- 1 jalapeno chile en escabeche or regular canned, minced jalapeno
- 1/4 c. cilantro, snipped

DIRECTIONS

Use a fork the mash the avocados with lemon juice so that it is lumpy. Add salsa, sour cream, onion, garlic, salt, jalapeno chile, and cilantro.

GUACAMOLE BURGERS

INGREDIENTS

- 1 lb. ground beef
- 1/2 c. Old El Paso taco or tostada shells, crushed
- 1/3 c. milk
- 1/2 tsp. onion salt
- 15 sm. tomatoes, peeled, seeded, chopped
- 1 c. guacamole
- 5 hamburger buns, split, toasted & buttered

DIRECTIONS

Combine the beef, crushed taco shells, milk, and onion salt. Make the mixture into patties, and grill for 5 minutes on each side. Add tomato, while stirring. Spread guacamole over each burger, and serve on buns.

CAULIFLOWER SALAD WITH GUACAMOLE DRESSING

INGREDIENTS

- 1 hard raw cauliflower (about 2 lb.)
- 1/2 c. green pepper, thinly sliced
- 1/2 c. red pepper, thinly sliced
- 3/4 c. homemade oil & vinegar dressing
- 1 head Romaine lettuce
- 1 lg. cucumber, sliced
- 4 tomatoes, sliced

DIRECTIONS

Cut the cauliflower into thin slices, and mix with the peppers. Toss with oil and vinegar dressing. Chill for 2 hours.

Decorate a plate with overlapping layers of romaine lettuce, tomatoes, and cucumbers. Add the cauliflower mixture to the center, and serve with guacamole dressing.

DRESSING:

- 2 tbsp. oil & vinegar dressing
- 2 ripe avocados, peeled & chopped
- 1 sm. tomato, peeled & chopped
- 2 tbsp. mild green chilies, chopped
- 2 tbsp. onion, grated
- 1 tsp. salt

Add the avocados, oil, and vinegar to a blender, and mix until smooth to make the dressing. In a bowl, mix in remaining ingredients. Chill before serving.

GREEN PEA GUACAMOLE

INGREDIENTS

For those who love guacamole dip but cannot afford all the saturated fat of avocado, this dish offers the best of both worlds.

- 3 green peas, fresh or frozen
- 1 c. red onions
- 2 tbsp. lemon juice
- 2 tsp. garlic, minced
- 1 tsp. ground cumin
- 1/4 tsp. fresh ground black pepper
- 1/8 tsp. cayenne pepper
- Salt

DIRECTIONS

Defrost the peas if frozen. If fresh, steam them before using. Use a blender to puree the peas with lemon juice, onions, garlic, cumin, and black pepper. Season to taste with cayenne and salt.

FRESH VEGETABLES WITH GUACAMOLE DIP

INGREDIENTS

- 2 sm. avocados
- 2 tbsp. lemon juice
- 2 tbsp. green onions, chopped
- 2 tsp. salt
- 1 tsp. sugar
- 1/2 tsp. hot pepper sauce
- Dash pepper
- 2 green peppers, cut into thin strips
- 2 red peppers, cut into thin strips
- 2 (8 oz.) bags or 2 bunches white radishes, cut into thin strips

DIRECTIONS

Mix the avocados, lemon juice, green onions, salt, sugar, hot sauce, and pepper in a blender until smooth. Chill before serving. Serve on a platter with green peppers, red peppers, and white radishes.

GUACAMOLE BOATS

INGREDIENTS

- 7 ripe avocados, peeled & seeded
- 2 tsp. garlic powder
- 2 tsp. onion salt
- 3 tbsp. picante sauce
- 1 tomato, chopped in sm. pieces
- 1 tbsp. lemon juice
- Salt & pepper
- 4 med. tomatoes
- Tortilla chips
- Lemon juice (opt.)

DIRECTIONS

Roughly mash the avocados so that they are chunky. Mix in garlic powder, salt, picante, tomato, and lemon juice. Season with salt and pepper. Take the 4 medium tomatoes, slice in half, scoop out pulp, and saw tooth the edges to make a decorative bowl. Put the mixture inside the tomato boats. Serve.

GUACAMOLE CHEESE DIP

INGREDIENTS

- 8 oz. Green Goddess Salad dressing (chilled)
- 3 med. avocados (peeled and mashed)
- 1 pkt. Guacamole dip mix
- 2 cans (4 1/2 oz. each) deveined tiny shrimp, drained and chilled
- 1 c. shredded Taco flavored cheese
- Few drops red pepper sauce, optional

DIRECTIONS

Blend all the ingredients together. Chill before serving.

HOLY GUACAMOLE

INGREDIENTS

- 2 ripe California avocados, peeled and diced
- 1 1/2 tbsp. lemon juice, preferably fresh
- 1-2 cloves garlic, minced
- 1 tsp. dried leaf basil, crushed
- 1/4 c. red pepper, finely diced
- 2 tbsp. your favorite salsa
- 1 1/2 tbsp. slivered almonds, coarsely chopped
- 2 tbsp. green onion, thinly sliced
- Dollop sour cream garnish
- 1/2 tsp. salt (optional)
- 1 tbsp. cilantro, minced (optional

DIRECTIONS

Blend 1 avocado with lemon juice, and add cilantro, garlic, basil, and salt. Use remaining avocado to dice and stir into the mixture. Stir in red pepper, salsa, green onion, and chopped almonds. Use sour cream to garnish. Serve.

KILLER GUACAMOLE

INGREDIENTS

- 4 lg. Hass avocados
- 2 med.-lg. tomatoes, diced
- 1 clove garlic, diced
- 1 onion, diced
- Salt and pepper to taste
- 4 oz. green chilies, diced
- 4 oz. black olives, sliced
- 2 tbsp. lemon juice
- 4 tbsp. hot salsa
- 2-4 jalapeno chilies (canned), diced
- 1 tbsp. parsley flakes
- 1 c. grated Cheddar or Monterey Jack cheese

DIRECTIONS

Mash the avocados with lemon juice until smooth. Mix in the diced tomatoes, garlic, onion, green chilies, salsa, and parsley. Season with salt and pepper. Add desired amount of jalapeno peppers. Chill to serve.

MEXICAN WON TONS W/GUACAMOLE

INGREDIENTS

- 1 pkg. won ton shells
- 20 oz. shredded Monterey Jack cheese w/jalapenos
- 3 each Haas California avocado or 1 lg. Florida avocado
- 2 lg. limes, juiced
- 1 tsp. salt
- 1/2 tsp. red pepper
- 2 tsp. sour cream
- 1 bottle corn oil

DIRECTIONS

Put ½ tsp. of cheese in the middle of each wonton wrapper. Fold over corners, and pinch to seal. In a wok filled with oil, deep fry the won tons until turn golden brown. Drain.

Blend together the avocado with all remaining ingredients. Serve as a dip with the won tons.

7 LAYER GUACAMOLE DIP

Add 1 can of refried bean evenly over the bottom of a 13x9 inch pan.

Crush the avocados with 1 tbsp. of lemon juice until smooth. Make a second layer in the dish.

Blend 1 cup sour cream, ½ cup mayonnaise, and 1 package of Old El Paso seasoning mix. Spread over second layer.

Sprinkle 1 bunch of chopped green onions over the top.

AUTHENTIC GUACAMOLE DIP

INGREDIENTS

- 2 ripe avocados, mashed
- 1 tbsp. onion, minced
- 1 garlic clove, mashed
- 1/4 tsp. chili powder
- 1/4 tsp. salt
- Dash of pepper
- 1/3 c. mayonnaise
- 6 slices crisp bacon, crumbled

DIRECTIONS

Puree the avocados in a blender. Mix in everything but the bacon and mayonnaise. Add avocado mixture to a bowl, and top with mayonnaise to seal. Crumble bacon over the top to serve.

BEST - EVER GUACAMOLE

INGREDIENTS

- 4 ripe avocados, mashed
- 1 med. Tomato, chopped
- 1 sm. Onion, chopped
- Salt
- Celery salt
- Pepper
- Ground cumin
- Lemon juice
- Prepared horseradish
- Picante sauce

DIRECTIONS

Blend together the avocados, tomato, and onion. Use salt, celery salt, pepper, cumin, lemon juice, horseradish, and picante to season to taste.

BEST GUACAMOLE DIP

INGREDIENTS

- 5 very ripe avocados
- 1 tomato, chopped
- 1/2 c. onion, chopped fine
- 2 tsp. lemon juice
- 1 tsp. garlic salt
- 1 c. sour cream
- Salt & pepper to taste

DIRECTIONS

Mash the avocados with lemon juice. Stir in sour cream, and seasonings. Stir until creamy. Mix in onion and tomato to serve.

BLENDER GUACAMOLE

INGREDIENTS

- 2 ripe, avocados, sliced
- 2 tbsp. onion
- 1 1/4 tbsp. lemon juice
- 1/2 tsp. chili powder
- 1/3 c. mayonnaise
- 1 sm. tomato

DIRECTIONS

In a blender, mix all ingredients until smooth. Serve.

"BEST IN THE WEST" GUACAMOLE

INGREDIENTS

- 1 ripe avocado
- 1/2 med. tomato, chopped
- 1 green onion, chopped
- 1 tsp. fresh lemon juice
- Several drops Tabasco sauce
- Salt and pepper to taste
- 1 sm. clove garlic, minced (optional)
- Generous tsp. fresh coriander, chopped (optional)

DIRECTIONS

Mash the avocado with a fork in a bowl. Mix with lemon juice, and then add remaining ingredients. Season with Tabasco, salt, and pepper.

BROCCOLI GUACAMOLE

INGREDIENTS

- 1 c. broccoli, chopped, cooked and cooled
- 1/4 c. sour cream
- 1/4 c. mayonnaise
- 2 tbsp. Parmesan cheese, grated
- 1/4 c. Cheddar cheese, grated
- 1 tsp. green onion, minced
- 1/4 to 1/2 tsp. curry powder
- 1/4 tsp. salt
- 1 squeeze lemon juice

DIRECTIONS

Use a blender to puree all ingredients. Chill before serving.

CHILLED GUACAMOLE SOUP

INGREDIENTS

- 2 lg. avocados, peeled and seeded
- 3 med. tomatoes, peeled and chopped
- 2 tbsp. green pepper, chopped
- 2 tbsp. green onion, chopped
- 2 tbsp. celery, chopped
- 1 tbsp. lemon juice
- Hot pepper sauce
- 1 1/4 c. chicken broth
- Salt
- Few drops of green food color (optional)
- 4 to 6 oz. vodka (optional)

DIRECTIONS

Mix 1 avocado, tomatoes, green pepper, celery, green onion, lemon juice, and hot pepper sauce in a blender until smooth. Pour in broth. Season with salt, and continue to blend. Chill before serving. Scoop remaining avocados with a melon baller, and put into soup.

CHICKEN - RICE SALAD WITH GUACAMOLE DRESSING

INGREDIENTS

- 2 1/2 c. cooked rice
- 2 lg. chicken breasts, cooked & cut into pieces
- 1 (10 oz.) pkg. frozen peas, thawed but not cooked
- 1/2 c. onion, chopped
- 1 c. celery, chopped
- 1 tsp. salt
- 1 tsp. pepper
- 1/2 c. mayonnaise
- Dash hot sauce
- Chopped pimentos, if desired

DIRECTIONS

Mix all ingredients together to make the salad, and chill.

DRESSING:

- 1 lg. avocado, mashed
- 1/2 c. mayonnaise
- 1/2 tsp. Worcestershire sauce
- 1 c. sour cream
- 1/2 tsp. grated onion
- 1/4 tsp. garlic salt
- 1/2 tsp. salt
- Dash hot sauce

In a blender, mix all ingredients to make the dressing. Chill and toss with salad to serve.

CHISOLM TRAIL GUACAMOLE

INGREDIENTS

- 3 med. ripe avocados
- 1 (8 oz.) pkg. cream cheese
- 1 tbsp. lemon juice
- 1 tsp. garlic salt
- 1/4 tsp. Tabasco sauce
- 1/2 tsp. Worcestershire sauce
- 1/2 tsp. Lawry's seasoning salt
- 1/2 tsp. onion salt
- 1 med. onion
- 1 med. tomato

DIRECTIONS

Mash together the avocados with lemon juice. Mix in the softened cream cheese until blended well. Dice the onion and tomato to add to the mixture. Mix in the sauces and seasonings. Chill to serve.

CHUNKY GUACAMOLE SALAD

INGREDIENTS

- 3 ripe avocados, peeled, cut into 1/2" cubes
- 2 tbsp. plus an additional
- 1/3 c. fresh lime juice
- 6 ripe plum tomatoes, each cut into 8 pieces
- 3 tbsp. red onion, chopped
- 1 tbsp. Dijon style mustard
- 1 tsp. garlic, finely minced
- 1/2 c. Spanish extra-virgin olive oil
- 3 tbsp. fresh cilantro, chopped
- 3 tbsp. oregano & Italian parsley
- 1 c. slice black olives

DIRECTIONS

Sprinkle the avocado cubes with 2 tbsps. of lime juice in a bowl. Add the tomatoes, red onions, and black olives.

Blend 1/3 cup lime juice, mustard, and garlic in a separate bowl. Drip olive oil over the top, and stir to whisk. Season with salt and pepper. Toss 1/3 cup of the dressing with the salad. Chill remaining dressing for another meal. Garnish with fresh herbs, cilantro, oregano, and parsley to serve.

ENSALADA DE GUACAMOLE

INGREDIENTS

- 6 slices bacon
- 3 tbsp. vegetable oil
- 1 tbsp. vinegar
- 1/2 tsp. salt
- 1/8 tsp. pepper
- 3 drops red pepper sauce
- 2 med. avocados, peeled and cubed
- 2 med. tomatoes, chopped
- 1 sm. onion, chopped
- Salad greens

DIRECTIONS

In a pan, heat the oil and fry the bacon. Drain the bacon on a paper towel, and then break it into pieces. Blend together the oil, vinegar, salt, pepper, and red pepper sauce. Toss the mixture with the avocados, and then stir in the bacon, tomatoes, and onion. Chill for 2 hours. Serve over fresh greens.

GARBONZO GUACAMOLE DIP

INGREDIENTS

- 1 (8 oz.) garbanzo beans, drained
- 2 tbsp. lemon juice
- 1 garlic clove, minced
- 1/2 c. red onion or yellow
- 1 sm. ripe avocado, peeled and cubed
- 1/2 c. dairy sour cream
- 1 (4 oz.) can green mild chilies, diced and undrained
- Dash of hot pepper sauce and cumin
- 1 med. tomato, chopped
- Tortillas, chips, olives, cheese

DIRECTIONS

Mix the beans, lemon juice, and garlic in a blender for 10 seconds. Then, add everything but the tomatoes. Blend until smooth for another 45 seconds.

Chill before serving. Used chopped tomatoes to garnish.

GREEN CHILI PEPPER GUACAMOLE

INGREDIENTS

- 4 avocados, mashed
- 1/2 c. green chili peppers, finely chopped
- 1/4 c. onion, minced
- 1 tsp. salt
- 1/4 c. lemon juice

DIRECTIONS

Blend all ingredients together. Chill covered before serving.

GRINGO GUACAMOLE

INGREDIENTS

- 4 lg. ripe avocados
- 6 tbsp. lime juice
- 2 cloves garlic, minced
- 4 tbsp. fresh cilantro, chopped
- 6 canned green chiles, rinsed, seeded & chopped
- 2 med. tomatoes, peeled, seeded & chopped
- Minced jalapeno or serrano chiles to taste
- Salt
- Cilantro sprigs as garnish

DIRECTIONS

Mash the avocado with lime juice, garlic, cilantro, chiles, tomatoes, and jalapeno chiles. Season with salt. Use cilantro sprigs to garnish. Can be served with fried tortilla.

GUACAMOLE COCKTAIL SPREAD

INGREDIENTS

- 1 lg. avocado
- 1 tbsp. onion, grated
- 1 tbsp. chili sauce
- Dash cayenne pepper
- 1 clove garlic, grated
- 1/2 tsp. or more salt

DIRECTIONS

Slice the avocados in half, and scoop out fruit so that the skin stays intact. Mix all ingredients together with the avocado. Season to taste. Scoop mixture into avocado skins. Chill and serve.

GUACAMOLE CON CHILES

INGREDIENTS

- 2 lg. avocados, peel, seed & cut up
- 1 sm. tomato, peeled & cut up
- 1/2 sm. onion, cut up
- 2 or 3 canned green chili peppers, rinsed & seeded
- 2 tbsp. lemon juice
- 3/4 tsp. salt

DIRECTIONS

Mix the avocados, tomato, onion, chili peppers, lemon juice, and salt in a blender. Serve when well mixed.

GUACAMOLE COLOMBO

INGREDIENTS

- 1 lg. ripe avocado
- 1 c. tomato, chopped
- 1/4 c. green pepper, chopped
- 1 tsp. chili powder
- 1 tsp. onion salt
- 1 tbsp. lime juice
- 1 tbsp. olive oil
- 1 c. plain yogurt or sour cream

DIRECTIONS

Add yogurt to the mashed avocados so they keep longer.
Mix all ingredients together, and serve.

GUACAMOLE CREAM SOUP

INGREDIENTS

- 1 lg. avocado, peeled and pitted
- 1 slice onion
- 1 c. heavy cream
- 1 tsp. instant chicken base
- 1/2 tsp. salt
- 3 drops red pepper seasoning, optional
- 2 c. milk

DIRECTIONS

In a blender, mix the avocados with onion, and ½ cup cream. Add remaining cream, instant chicken base, seasoning, and milk to stir in. Chill before serving. Garnish with paprika.

GUACAMOLE DIP IN PUMPERNICKLE

INGREDIENTS

- 1 round loaf pumpernickel bread, unsliced
- 2 avocados
- 1 tomato, peeled and chopped
- 1 sm. onion, finely chopped
- 1/2 fresh squeezed lemon
- 1 clove garlic, minced
- Dash salt and pepper

DIRECTIONS

Scoop out the center of the pumpernickel bread by slicing off the top to make the bowl. Mash the avocados with lemon juice in a bowl. Add garlic, salt, pepper, and tomatoes. Once mixed, put the mixture into the center of the pumpernickel bowl. Put bread chunks to the side

DISCLAIMER AND/OR LEGAL NOTICES: Every effort has been made to accurately represent this book and it's potential. Results vary with every individual, and your results may or may not be different from those depicted. No promises, guarantees or warranties, whether stated or implied, have been made that you will produce any specific result from this book. Your efforts are individual and unique, and may vary from those shown. Your success depends on your efforts, background and motivation.

The material in this publication is provided for educational and informational purposes only and is not intended as medical advice. The information contained in this book should not be used to diagnose or treat any illness, metabolic disorder, disease or health problem. Always consult your physician or health care provider before beginning any nutrition or exercise program. Use of the programs, advice, and information contained in this book is at the sole choice and risk of the reader.

42783999R00074

Made in the USA
San Bernardino, CA
12 December 2016